SUPER SIMPLE BODY

INSIDE THE BRAIN

KARIN HALVORSON, M.D.

Consulting Editor, Diane Craig, M.A./Reading Specialist

A Division of ABDO

ABDO
Publishing Company

VISIT US AT WWW.ABDOPUBLISHING.COM

Published by ABDO Publishing Company, a division of
ABDO, P.O. Box 398166, Minneapolis, Minnesota 55439.
Copyright © 2013 by Abdo Consulting Group, Inc.
International copyrights reserved in all countries. No
part of this book may be reproduced in any form without
written permission from the publisher. Super SandCastle™
is a trademark and logo of ABDO Publishing Company.

Printed in the United States of America,
North Mankato, Minnesota
102012
012013

Editor: Liz Salzmann
Content Developer: Nancy Tuminelly
Cover and Interior Design: Anders Hanson, Mighty Media
Photo Credits: Shutterstock, Dorling Kindersley RF/Thinkstock,
Colleen Dolphin

Library of Congress Cataloging-in-Publication Data
Halvorson, Karin, 1979-
  Inside the brain / Karin Halvorson ; consulting editor, Diane Craig.
    p. cm. -- (Super simple body)
  ISBN 978-1-61783-609-1
  1. Brain--Juvenile literature. I. Title.
  QP376.H262 2013
  612.8'2--dc23
                    2012028763

Super SandCastle™ books are created by a team of professional
educators, reading specialists, and content developers around five
essential components—phonemic awareness, phonics, vocabulary,
text comprehension, and fluency—to assist young readers as they
develop reading skills and strategies and increase their general
knowledge. All books are written, reviewed, and leveled for guided
reading, early reading intervention, and Accelerated Reader®
programs for use in shared, guided, and independent reading
and writing activities to support a balanced approach to literacy
instruction.

NOTE TO ADULTS

THIS BOOK is all about encouraging children to learn the science of how their bodies work! Be there to help make science fun and interesting for young readers. Many activities are included in this book to help children further explore what they've learned. Some require adult assistance and/or permission. Make sure children have appropriate places where they can do the activities safely.

Children may also have questions about what they've learned. Offer help and guidance when they have questions. Most of all encourage them to keep exploring and learning new things!

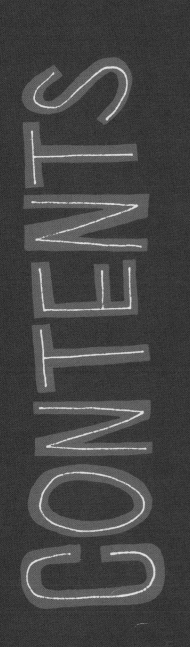

CONTENTS

YOUR BODY

YOUR BRAIN

You're amazing! So is your body!

Your body has a lot of different parts. Your eyes, ears, brain, stomach, lungs, and heart all work together every day. They keep you moving. Even when you don't realize it.

Your brain is a wonderful thing! It's in charge of everything in your body. You couldn't live without it. Your brain is working when you're solving math problems. It's working when you are running in the park. It's even working when you are asleep!

This book will help you learn about your brain. You'll discover how it works! Then try the fun activities. They'll help you explore your brain even more!

CAN YOU THINK OF OTHER WAYS THAT YOU USE YOUR BRAIN?

ALL ABOUT THE

BRAIN

Your brain is a very important organ. It is inside your head. Your brain lets you understand the world.

{ **FAST FACT** }

AN ADULT BRAIN IS
ABOUT THE SIZE OF
A GRAPEFRUIT.

SEEING

HEARING

SMELLING

TASTING

TOUCHING

You sense the world by seeing, hearing, smelling, tasting, and touching. Your senses have special nerves. They take messages from other parts of your body to your brain. Your brain figures out what they mean. That is how you understand the things you sense.

THE GROWING BRAIN

AT BIRTH your brain weighed 1 pound (.4 kg).
IN ELEMENTARY SCHOOL it weighs 2 pounds (.9 kg).
AS AN ADULT your brain will weigh 3 pounds (1.4 kg).

OH, THE NERVE!

Your skin is your largest sense organ. Its nerves go to the spinal cord (SPIN-UHL KORD). When something touches your skin, your nerves feel it. The nerves take **information** about the touch to your spinal cord. Your spinal cord sends the message to your brain. Your brain tells you what the touch felt like.

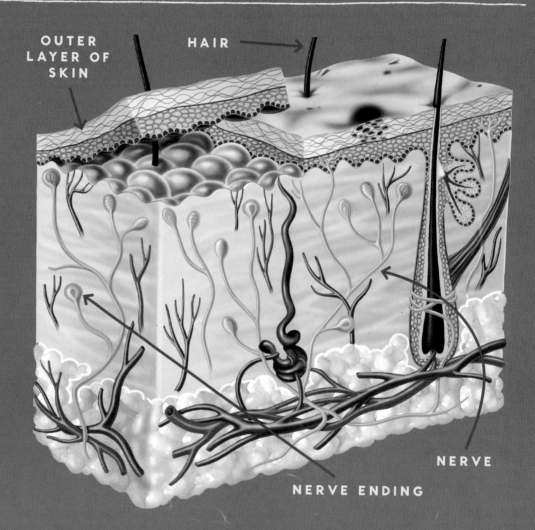

OUTER LAYER OF SKIN

HAIR

NERVE

NERVE ENDING

Your spinal cord is a group of nerves in your back. The bones in your spine protect your spinal cord. Your spinal cord connects to your brain stem.

REFLEX ACTION

Sometimes your spinal cord **reacts** to a touch without telling your brain. This is called a reflex. It helps you react faster. Reflexes are part of survival.

SPINAL CORD

NERVES

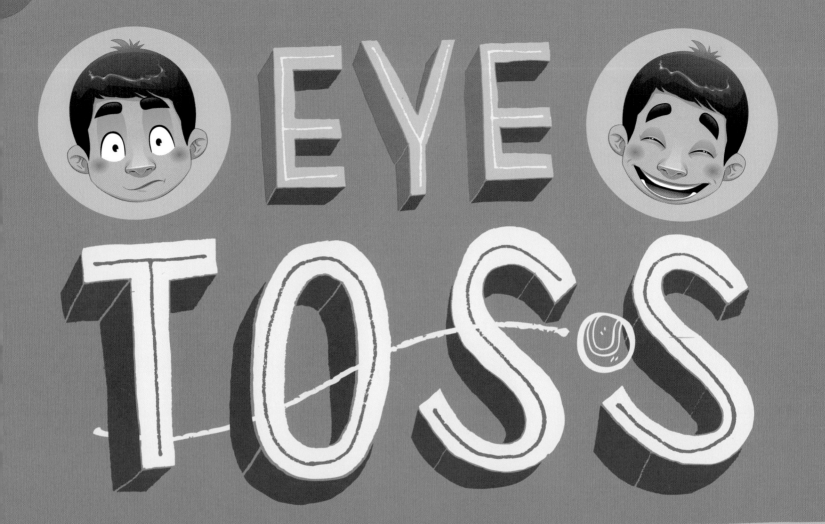

EYE TOSS

BLINK BEFORE YOU THINK!

WHAT YOU NEED: **PLASTIC WRAP, SCISSORS, TAPE MEASURE, 2 WOODEN DOWELS, TAPE, A FRIEND, TENNIS BALL**

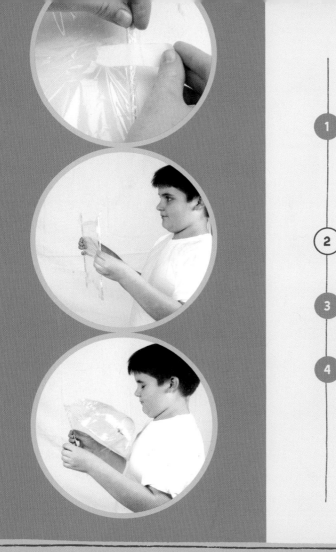

HOW TO DO IT

1. Tear off a piece of plastic wrap. It should be about 15 inches (38 cm) long. Place a wooden dowel along one end of the plastic wrap. Roll the plastic wrap over it a few times. Tape it in place.

2. Repeat step 1 at the other end of the plastic wrap.

3. Grab a dowel in each hand. Hold your arms out. Make sure the plastic wrap is tight and vertical.

4. Have a friend gently toss a tennis ball at the plastic wrap. Did you move? Did you **blink**? Try not to blink when your friend tosses the ball. Can you stop yourself? Switch places with your friend and see what he or she does!

WHAT'S HAPPENING?

Blinking is a reflex. People blink to protect their eyes. Even though your eyes were safe, your nerves took over for your brain!

REACTION ACTION

TEST YOUR REFLEXES!

WHAT YOU NEED: CHAIR, RUBBER HAMMER (OPTIONAL), A FRIEND

HOW TO DO IT

1 Sit in a chair. Make sure your feet don't touch the floor. Have a friend gently tap the front of your knee with the edge of one hand. Watch what happens.

2 Hold out your arm so your forearm hangs loosely. Have a friend tap the soft area just above your elbow. Watch what happens.

3 Repeat steps 1 and 2. This time, try to stop your **reactions**. Can you? Have your friend try too!

WHAT'S HAPPENING?

Your muscles have to be ready for action all the time! When your friend tapped your knee and your elbow, your body reacted without telling your brain! That's a reflex.

THE
BUSY BRAIN

Your brain stem is the bottom part of your brain. It connects to your spinal cord. It is like the secretary for your brain. Messages from your sense organs enter your brain through your brain stem. Your brain stem controls actions of your body that you don't think about.

Your brain stem has three parts.

The medulla (MUH-DUHL-UH) controls things such as breathing. It also controls your heartbeat.

The pons (PONZ) helps with breathing. Its other job is to help you sleep.

The midbrain helps with body movements and seeing.

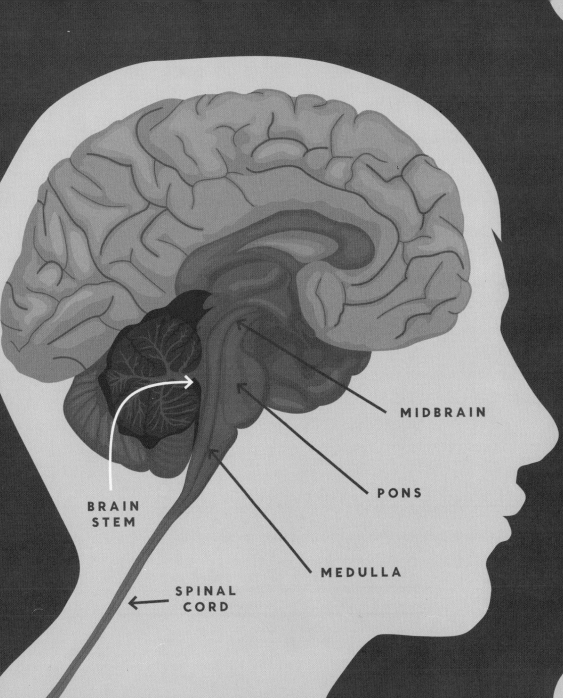

MIDBRAIN

PONS

BRAIN STEM

MEDULLA

SPINAL CORD

15

THE
LITTLE BRAIN
THAT COULD

Also at the bottom of your brain is your cerebellum (SER-UH-BEL-UHM). The name *cerebellum* means "little brain" in **Latin**.

Your cerebellum controls how muscles work together in your body. This helps you keep your balance. Balancing, walking, and even skateboarding are all controlled by your cerebellum.

CEREBELLUM

MUSCLE MANIA

Your cerebellum controls a lot of muscles!

You have **MORE THAN 630 MUSCLES** you can move.

Your **BIGGEST MUSCLE** is your gluteus maximus. That's your butt.

Your face has **30 DIFFERENT MUSCLES.** They help you show feelings such as anger and happiness.

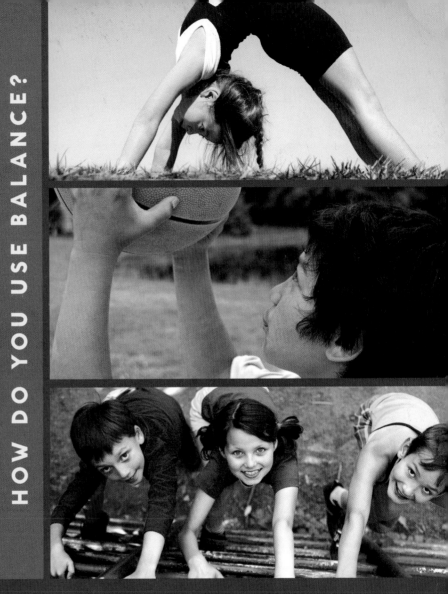

HOW DO YOU USE BALANCE?

CAN YOU THINK OF OTHER WAYS THAT YOUR MUSCLES WORK TOGETHER?

BALANCING ACTS

WALK THE LINE!

WHAT YOU NEED: TAPE MEASURE, MASKING TAPE, BLINDFOLD, BEANBAG, STOPWATCH, A FRIEND

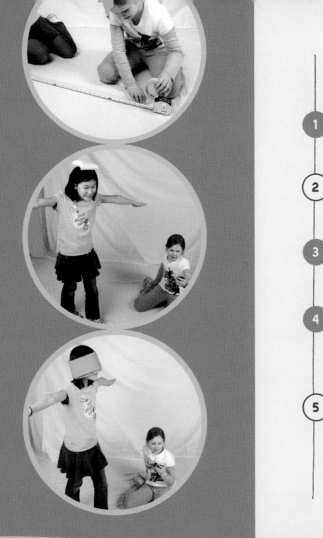

HOW TO DO IT

1. Use masking tape to make a 6-foot (2 m) line on the floor.

2. Walk along the line. Have your friend time how long it takes you.

3. Balance a beanbag on your head. Try walking the line again. Were you just as fast?

4. Try walking the line wearing a blindfold. Have your friend tell you when to stop. Were you slower? Why do you think you were?

5. Try other balancing acts. Hop the line on one foot. Or walk the line going backwards.

WHAT'S HAPPENING?

Your cerebellum is working overtime to keep you balanced! It helps you stay standing even when you can't use your senses, such as sight.

MIND CONTROL

THE SUPER CEREBRUM

Your cerebrum (SUH-REE-BRUHM) is the biggest part of your brain. It has a lot of folds and bumps. It also has two sides, the left and the right. They are connected by the corpus callosum (KOR-PUHS KUH-LOH-SUHM).

CEREBRUM

CORPUS CALLOSUM

Your cerebrum has a lot of jobs. It's in charge of your memories, **personality**, emotion, speech, and intelligence. Your cerebrum's biggest job is to help you do the things you decide to do. It is working when you brush your teeth, create art, and do your homework!

WHAT DID YOU DECIDE TO DO TODAY?

THERE ARE
TWO SIDES
TO EVERY BRAIN

The two sides of your cerebrum are called hemispheres. They are also called the left brain and right brain.

THE CORPUS CALLOSUM CONNECTS THE TWO SIDES

LEFT BRAIN

ORGANIZATION

LOGIC

MATHEMATICAL THINKING

VOCABULARY

REASON

GRAMMAR

THE RIGHT SIDE OF THE BODY

RIGHT BRAIN

CREATIVITY

IMAGINATION

ARTISTIC ABILITY

TONE OF VOICE

INTUITION

MUSICAL ABILITY

THE LEFT SIDE OF THE BODY

WHAT'S YOUR SIDE?

Everyone uses both of their cerebral hemispheres. But some people use one side more than the other. Which do you use more?

If you are LEFT-BRAINED it means you think more **logically**. You like doing math problems and organizing your room.

If you are RIGHT-BRAINED it means you think more creatively. You like art or music class and easily recognize people's faces.

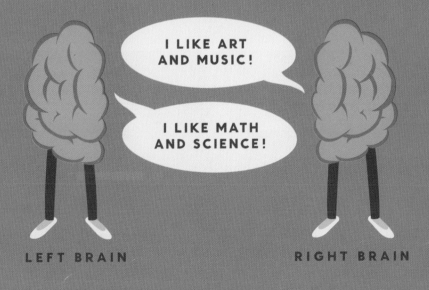

I LIKE ART AND MUSIC!

I LIKE MATH AND SCIENCE!

LEFT BRAIN

RIGHT BRAIN

COOL CHARACTER

THE FRONTAL LOBE

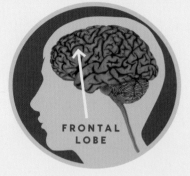

FRONTAL LOBE

The front part of your cerebrum is called the frontal lobe (FRUHN-TUHL LOHB). Your frontal lobe is in charge of your **personality**. It makes you who you are. It tells you right from wrong. It is also very important in understanding smells.

| PERSONALITY | RIGHT AND WRONG | SMELLING |

LISTEN HERE!

THE TEMPORAL LOBE

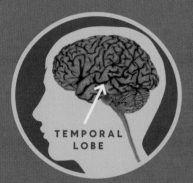

TEMPORAL LOBE

Your temporal (TEM-PUR-UHL) lobes are on each side of your cerebrum. They work to understand what you hear. They are also in charge of what you say. Deep inside each temporal lobe is a hippocampus (HI-PUH-KAM-PUHS). That is your memory center.

HEARING	SPEAKING	MEMORY

GET TOGETHER!

THE PARIETAL LOBE

PARIETAL LOBE

Your parietal (PUH-RYE-UH-TUHL) lobes are on the upper sides of your brain. Your parietal lobes are your **integration** (IN-TI-GRAY-SHUHN) centers. That's where your brain organizes the messages that your nerves send it. It deals with temperature, touch, and objects.

TEMPERATURE	TOUCH	OBJECTS

EYE SPY

THE OCCIPITAL LOBE

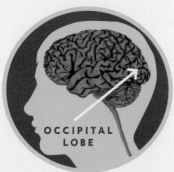

OCCIPITAL LOBE

At the very back of your brain is your occipital (AHK-SI-PUH-TUHL) lobe. Your occipital lobe is your vision (VIZH-UHN) center. It helps you know what you are seeing. Your occipital lobe lets you see the difference between letters of the alphabet. Without it, you couldn't use your eyes to read!

CAN YOU SEE THE NUMBER?

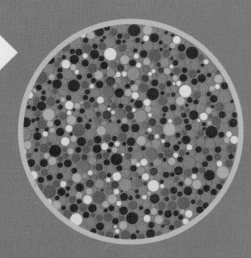

Some people can't tell the difference between some colors. This is called being color-blind. The colors red and green can look the same to someone who is color-blind.

Can you see the number in the circle?

COLOR CRAZY

DOUBLE YOUR VISION!

WHAT YOU NEED: BLACK MARKER, RED MARKER, YELLOW MARKER, BLUE MARKER, GREEN MARKER, PAPER, STOPWATCH, A FRIEND

HOW TO DO IT

1 Write a list of colors with a black marker. They can be in any order.

2 On a second sheet of paper write a list of colors using colored markers. Make sure each word is not the same color it is written in.

3 Have your friend read the first list out loud. Time how long it takes. Then have your friend read the second list. Did it take longer? Did your friend read all of the words correctly?

4 Try it yourself with your friend timing you! Which list was harder?

WHAT'S HAPPENING?

Your occipital lobe helps you understand what you see. But sometimes it gets mixed up! Sometimes your eyes see the color first and read the word second!

THINKING CAP

CREATE A MAP OF YOUR BRAIN!

WHAT YOU NEED: NEWSPAPER, BALLOON, BOWL, MOD PODGE, FOAM BRUSH, WHITE PAPER, SCISSORS, ACRYLIC PAINT PENS, WHITE STICKERS, BLACK MARKER

HOW TO DO IT

1. Cover your work area with newspaper. Tear extra newspaper into strips. Then blow up a balloon until it's about the size of your head.

2. Set the balloon in a bowl to keep it upright. Brush a coat of Mod Podge over the top half of the balloon. Cover the Mod Podge with newspaper strips. Put another coat of Mod Podge over the strips. Let the Mod Podge dry.

3. Repeat step 2 three more times. Use strips of white paper for the last layer. Let the Mod Podge dry completely.

4. Pop the balloon. Cut along the edge of the paper to make it even. Use acrylic paint pens to color the different parts of the brain. Let the paint dry. Use stickers to label the parts.

WHAT'S HAPPENING?

You made a model of your brain! Put the cap on your head. Try naming the parts of the brain without looking. Say the name of the part, then point to it on the cap.

BLINK – to quickly shut and open the eyes.

INFORMATION – something known about an event or subject.

INTEGRATION – the process of combining a lot of things into one.

LATIN – the language of ancient Rome.

LOGIC – sensible thinking or reasoning.

PERSONALITY – the special characteristics of a person or an animal.

REACT – to do something in response to something learned or sensed.

GLOSSARY